Pocket Timeline of
Islamic
Civilizations

Nicholas Badcott

INTERLINK BOOKS
An imprint of Interlink Publishing Group, Inc.
www.interlinkbooks.com

For my parents

First American edition published 2009 by

INTERLINK BOOKS
An imprint of Interlink Publishing Group, Inc.
46 Crosby Street, Northampton, Massachusetts 01060
www.interlinkbooks.com

Library of Congress Cataloging-in-Publication Data
available

ISBN-13: 978-1-56656-758-9

Book design by Crayon Design
Printed and bound in Malaysia by Tien Wah Press Ltd

To request our complete 40-page full-color catalog,
please call us toll free at 1-800-238-LINK
or visit our website at www.interlinkbooks.com.

Dating Systems

From early Islamic times, Muslims have dated events from the day of the Prophet Muhammad's migration from Mecca to Medina in AD 622. This is known as the *Hijra*, so Muslim years are usually referred to by the letters AH, standing for "after the *Hijra*." In this book, the familiar Christian dating system is used, with events numbered from year AD 1, the traditional date of the birth of Jesus Christ. The letters AD in front stand for *Anno Domini*, "in the year of our Lord." In the top panel of the Timeline, AH dates are also given.

Illustration Acknowledgements

Photographs were taken by the Dept of Photography and Imaging at the British Museum and are copyright © The Trustees of the British Museum unless otherwise indicated.

5 below: © Spectrum/Imagestate.
8 below: © Jonathan Tubb.
9 above: © Terry J. Alcorn.
12 above: © St John Simpson.
13 above: © V&A Images,
            Victoria and Albert Museum.
13 centre: © David Pedre.
15 below: © Adrian Beesley.
16 above: © Khalili Collection.

17 below right: © Richard Ashworth/
            Robert Harding.
18 above and 21 above: © The British Library.
21 below left and right: © Nicholas Badcott.
25 above: © iStockphoto.
25 below: © Bettman/CORBIS.
26 below: © Irtati Hasan Wibisono.
31 above: © iStockphoto.
Timeline (Mecca pilgrims): © Aidar Ayazbayev.

CONTENTS

EARLY ISLAMIC WORLD

AD 570 TO 660 ISLAM was introduced to the world in Arabia in the early seventh century AD by the Prophet Muhammad. Muhammad was born in about 570 in Mecca, in what is now Saudi Arabia. Muslims believe that he was the last in a long line of prophets. They also believe that Allah (God) revealed the Quran, the Muslim holy book, to Muhammad through his messenger the archangel Jibrail (Gabriel).

An archangel in a 15th century manuscript from Iraq. Muslims believe that Allah sent the archangel Jibrail (Gabriel) to reveal the Quran to the Prophet Muhammad.

These revelations began when Muhammad went to Mount Hira near Mecca to meditate in 610. The archangel appeared and asked him to recite but Muhammad said he could not. He was repeatedly asked to do this until finally, miraculously he was able to recite the words of Allah. The language in which Muhammad spoke was Arabic.

Muhammad shared Allah's messages with his family and friends but later began to speak publicly about them. However, some people in Mecca felt threatened by his words and persecuted him and his followers. As a result, in 622 they moved to Medina. This journey or migration is known as the *Hijra* and marks the beginning of the Muslim calendar or dating system. In Medina, Muhammad's house became the centre of the first community of Muslims.

While he was in Medina many people came to support the Prophet and fight for Islam. In 624 his followers defeated a larger Meccan army at Badr in Arabia. Six years later Muhammad's forces captured Mecca.

Muhammad died in 632. Abu Bakr, his father-in-law and one of his most trusted supporters, became the head of the Muslim community. He was the first *khalifa* (caliph) meaning 'successor' or 'deputy', and the first of the 'rightly-guided' caliphs.

A sword-fight from a detail on a brass ewer made in 1232 in northern Iraq. The earliest Muslim armies used similar weapons and were extremely successful in battle.

By the death of Muhammad, Islam was established in much of western Arabia, including Mecca and Medina. Over the following decades, Arab armies carried Islam beyond Arabia and into lands previously controlled by the Byzantines in the west and the Sasanians in the east.

The Kaaba in Mecca is the holiest place in Islam and the main goal of Muslim pilgrims. The granite, cube-like structure containing the Black Stone (possibly a meteorite fragment), is faced by Muslims from wherever they are praying in the world and is covered with the *kiswa*, a black silk curtain. Muslim tradition suggests that the Prophet Ibrahim (Abraham) and his son Ismail (Ishmael) built the Kaaba.

The Kaaba in Mecca was a shrine for the worship of local gods before it became the holiest place in the Islamic world.

A page from a Quran copied in Egypt or Syria in the 14th century. The title for the next chapter appears in the decorative band at the bottom of the page.

The Quran was memorized by Muhammad and his followers and shared orally. However, following Muhammad's death, Muslim leaders were worried Allah's message would be lost or become confused over time so it was decided to write it out. It is thought that the Caliph Umar (ruled 634–44) began this process. Because it is believed that the Quran contains the actual words of God in Arabic, when the Quran is copied the writing should be as beautiful as possible. From the late seventh century, Muslim calligraphers began developing a series of scripts or lettering styles to copy the Quran.

Before Muhammad died, 'five pillars' or essential duties in the life of a Muslim were established. The first is *Shahada,* the declaration of faith, 'there is no god but Allah, and Muhammad is the Messenger of Allah'; the second is *Salah,* or ritual prayer, five times a day facing towards the Kaaba; the third is *Zakat,* the payment of money to charity or for public benefit; the fourth is *Sawm,* or fasting during the month of Ramadan; and the fifth is *Hajj,* or pilgrimage to Mecca.

This compass was used to find the direction of Mecca in Saudi Arabia for prayer. Muslims pray five times a day facing the Kaaba in Mecca.

THE UMAYYADS

THE UMAYYAD FAMILY of the Arab Quraysh tribe took control of the Islamic empire following the murder of Ali ibn Abi Talib, the fourth caliph and the Prophet Muhammad's cousin and son-in-law. Muawiya became the first Umayyad caliph in 661.

Ali had been unpopular with some Muslims, who believed that the caliph should be the person most able to maintain the *Sunna* or teachings and actions of the Prophet. They became known as the people of the *Sunna* or 'Sunni Muslims'. Other Muslims thought that only someone related to the Prophet, such as Ali and his descendants, should lead the Islamic community. They were known as 'Shia Muslims', or people from the party or *Shia* of Ali.

A stucco (plaster) plaque showing a *senmurv* or dog-headed bird from a building in Iran, 7th-8th century. The *senmurv* was a mythical creature from Sasanian Iran. It continued to be popular after the Muslim Arab invasion in the mid-7th century.

The power of the Umayyad state was centred on the capital Damascus in Syria. From here, their army continued to expand Muslim rule west across North Africa and east into Central Asia and India. Each province of the empire had a local governor. By 700 Umayyad rule was strengthened by the creation of a new generation of administrators with Arabic as the official state language.

A gold *dinar* with a standing caliph. From the 690s, the Umayyads began minting coins with Arabic writing and no figures.

The earliest coins from the Islamic world adopted the figural designs of the Byzantines and Sasanians. The so-called 'standing caliph' may represent the Umayyad Caliph Abd al-

Dinar of Abd al-Malik from 696–7, after the coin reform.

Malik (reigned 685–705), wearing an Arab headcloth and robes and carrying a sword. Under this caliph in the 690s there was a revolution in coin design in order to emphasize the importance of the Quran and the Arabic language.

As Islam spread, the Arab Muslims absorbed ideas from the people and cultures that became part of the empire. Although power changed hands, the new regime adopted pre-Islamic court ceremonies and administrative and financial systems. In addition, craft techniques, architectural features and decorative styles from across the empire gradually shaped Islamic material culture.

Pottery oil lamp from Syria, 8th century.

Umayyad rulers lived in large cities like Damascus but also built palaces in rural Syria, Jordan and Palestine, with all the essential features of the time like bathhouses, mosques and storage rooms. These 'desert palaces' were often decorated with fine sculptures, stucco carvings and mosaic floors and may have provided a place for the rulers to relax away from city life.

Qusayr Amra, an Umayyad desert palace in Jordan.

The Umayyads carried out an extensive building programme, including the Dome of the Rock in Jerusalem and the Great Mosque in Damascus. Jerusalem was captured by Muslim forces in 639. Some time afterwards, the Umayyad Caliph Abd al-Malik ordered the Dome of the Rock to be built. Completed in about 692, it is the oldest Islamic building to survive in its original form. Its circular dome sits on an octagonal base and is supported by twelve pillars and four piers. The outside of the dome is covered in gold leaf, and the inside is decorated with mosaic tiles. The building has been renovated many times and it remains a place of pilgrimage for Muslims.

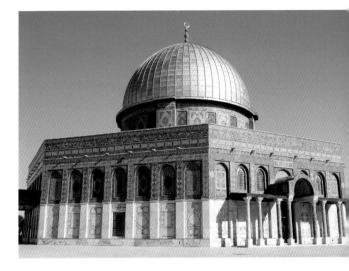

The Dome of the Rock in Jerusalem. In Islamic tradition, Muhammad was carried to Jerusalem and then taken up to visit heaven on a winged horse. This is known as the 'Night Journey'.

Resistance to Umayyad leadership had developed among Shia supporters of Husayn, the son of Ali the fourth caliph, but it was crushed in 680. However, by 700, the Umayyad leadership had become unpopular for their extravagant lifestyle and also unpopular with Persian Muslims, who felt they were being discriminated against. In 750 the Umayyads lost power in a rebellion that began in eastern Iran.

This astrolabic quadrant was used to determine the time for prayers at the Great Mosque, Damascus. The mosque was built by the Umayyads in the early 8th century.

THE ABBASIDS

THE REBELS who had defeated the Umayyads in 750 brought the Abbasids, an Arab clan, to power. The Abbasids had received support because they were descended from the Prophet Muhammad's uncle, al-Abbas.

A few years after the Abbasid dynasty took control of the Islamic empire, its second caliph al-Mansur (reigned 754–775) started building a new capital at Baghdad, in what is now modern Iraq. He did this for many reasons, but particularly because the site was at the crossroads of several important overland trade-routes. It was also close to the Tigris and Euphrates rivers, which connected to the Persian Gulf and the Indian Ocean.

A page from De Materia Medica by the ancient writer Dioscorides in Arabic, possibly from Baghdad, Iraq, 1224. Books in Latin and Greek were translated at the 'House of Wisdom' in Abbasid Baghdad.

The high quality of Abbasid gold *dinars* (coins) attracted many merchants to Baghdad and the city became a rich trading centre, with goods arriving from as far away as China, India and East Africa. Islamic silver *dirham* coins found in Britain and Scandinavia show that trade between the Muslim world and Europe was also developing from this time. Goods came to Baghdad from across the world. A ninth-century guide to imports lists tigers, silk, slaves, armour and sugarcane as coming into the city at the time. There were many specialized markets, including ones for flowers, gold and books.

Abbasid potters excelled at making both luxury and everyday ceramics. For example, they decorated pots with a special technique called 'lustre', giving them the appearance of precious metals such as gold or silver. Using lustre on ceramics was an invention of Arab potters in Iraq as early as the ninth century. Considerable knowledge of chemistry was needed to create it. The pottery was so popular that it was traded across the Islamic world and farther afield to Africa, India and Sri Lanka. It is likely that craftsmen took the 'lustre secret' with them as they travelled to new places. Later, rich and powerful families of Europe ordered it for their tables and even had their coats of arms added.

A 9th-century jug with lustre decoration. Lustre was very popular and the technique spread from Iraq to Iran, Egypt and Spain.

In the collections of the British Museum is a fascinating coin from Britain. Offa, the Anglo-Saxon king of Mercia (reigned 757–96), copied the gold *dinars* made in Iraq at the time of caliph al-Mansur. Could it be that he wanted to share the trade wealth in the Mediterranean? Abbasid *dinars* were very popular due to their high gold content. However, it seems that the British engraver did not understand the Arabic script. The name and title OFFA REX has been put on upside down in relation to the Arabic writing.

Gold imitation *dinar* of King Offa of Mercia in Britain. It is not known why an Anglo-Saxon king had a copy made of a coin from Abbasid Iraq.

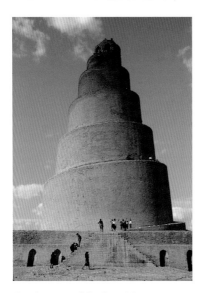

Spiral minaret of the Great Mosque at Samarra, Iraq.

A 9th century fragment of wall-painting from the harem baths at Samarra.

When the Abbasid rulers had trouble with their soldiers they decided to move the capital. The new capital city of Samarra, meaning 'Happy is he who sees it', was built from 836 on the river Tigris in Iraq. The city grew to twenty-five miles in length. There were palaces, baths, pools, gardens, polo grounds and race-courses. The walls of the palaces were painted with large scenes of hunters, dancers and drinkers. Special decorative techniques were used, like stucco plasterwork and mosaic tiling. The Abbasids abandoned the city after only about fifty years.

From an early stage, the caliph's power was limited. In order to rule in the distant parts of the empire, he had to use governors who could collect taxes and make their own decisions. Little by little these governors became more and more independent. However, although Baghdad was captured and controlled by other dynasties from 945, the caliphs lived on in the city until the arrival of the Mongols in 1258.

EARLY ISLAMIC SPAIN

MUSLIM contact with Spain began in the early eighth century when Berber soldiers raided from North Africa. Later, a strong Arab force invaded, seizing city after city from the Christian Visigoth rulers, and continued north into France until 732, when it was stopped near Tours by the Franks led by Charles Martel.

This ivory box was made for the daughter of Caliph Abd al-Rahman III in about 962.

In 756 Abd al-Rahman, an Umayyad prince who had escaped the Abbasid revolt, took control in Spain and developed Cordoba as his capital. The city – with its paved streets, lighting, running water, gardens and baths – was unrivalled in Europe during this period.

In early Islamic Spain, Muslims, Jews and Christians lived as neighbours and communicated in Arabic. Encouraged by Umayyad rulers, the arts and sciences flourished and Muslim and other scholars studied together in Cordoba and shared new ideas.

Inside the Mezquita or Great Mosque in Cordoba in Spain.

In the early eleventh century, Umayyad power declined and rebel soldiers sacked the palaces. Spain was then divided among the *Taifa* or 'party kings' who ruled from the cities of Malaga, Seville, Granada, Toledo and Valencia.

Astrolabes like this were developed by Muslim scientists to find the time and the direction in which to pray. Astrolabes were introduced to Christian Europe in the 10th century from Islamic Spain.

THE FATIMIDS

A Fatimid gold and enamel pendant. Fatimid jewellery resembled that of the Byzantines in its use of materials, shapes and decorative techniques.

THE FATIMIDS were a Shia movement which appeared in Tunisia, North Africa in 909. The dynasty was named after Fatima, the daughter of the Prophet Muhammad, who was married to Ali, the fourth caliph. The Fatimids occupied Egypt in 969 and founded al-Qahira (Cairo), meaning 'the victorious', as their capital.

The wealth of the Fatimids was based on local agriculture, fine crafts, and international trade. They controlled the trade-routes with Africa south of the Sahara, providing access to

Ivory chess-pieces from Egypt or Sicily, 10th–12th century. Chess was introduced into the Islamic world via Sasanian Iran.

precious raw materials like gold, rock crystal and ivory. From these their artists and craftsmen created beautiful objects that were traded around the Mediterranean and Red Sea.

Although little evidence remains today, the Fatimids were famous for their luxurious palaces, which were like treasure-houses. An inventory from al-Mustansir's reign (1036–94) includes precious stones, sacks of musk from Tibet and a golden peacock studded with jewels. Fatimid power was deliberately expressed through elaborate public ceremonies and processions when the caliph, carrying special regalia, would ride through the streets of Cairo to celebrate a special event.

The Fatimids claimed that, as descendants of Ali, they were the true leaders of Islam. As a result, they systematically campaigned to try to undermine the Sunni Abbasid caliphate in Iraq. Missionaries were specially trained in Cairo and sent out across the Abbasid empire and beyond to spread the teachings of Shia Islam. They also worked to encourage rebellion, and for a time the Fatimids controlled the holy cities of Mecca and Medina.

Christian Europe began the counter-attack against the Muslim powers in the Mediterranean in the eleventh century. This started with Italian attacks on Muslim pirates, included the gradual reconquest of Spain, and continued with the Norman conquest of Sicily. With the Muslims in the Middle East divided, the Christian Crusaders were able to fight their way down through Syria, capturing Jerusalem from the Fatimids in 1099.

The Fatimid dynasty gradually went into decline after losing Syria and Palestine to the Seljuqs (see page 16) and Crusaders.

Marble *kilga* were designed to hold large earthenware water jars. These porous jars cooled and filtered the water as it gradually seeped through into the basin.

Rock crystal bottle in the shape of a lion. Rock crystal came from sub-Saharan Africa. The Fatimids controlled trade routes across the Sahara and had links to East and Southern Africa, via the Red Sea and the Indian Ocean.

The al-Azhar Mosque was built as the main mosque in Cairo and as a centre for religious instruction. Today, it still functions as a mosque. Its teaching facilities have expanded into a fully-fledged modern university.

15

THE SELJUQS

Model of the Seljuq ruler Tughril Beg at prayer. In 1055 Tughril Beg captured Baghdad and made himself the protector of the Abbasid caliph.

Objects belonging to an important Seljuq courtier, found at Nihavand, western Iran, 11–12th century.

AD **1038** TO **1307**

The SELJUQS were descended from the Turkish nomadic tribes of Central Asia who converted to Islam in the late tenth century. They gradually took control of Iran, Mesopotamia and part of Afghanistan. Later, the empire expanded to include Syria and Anatolia.

Like other Turkic peoples, the Seljuqs had migrated southwards to Iran in the late tenth and early eleventh centuries to serve in the army of the Ghaznavid dynasty. In the 1030s, these 'Great Seljuqs' rebelled, drove out their masters and ruled in the region from 1038 to 1194.

In 1038, the Great Seljuqs captured Nishapur, in north-east Iran, making it their residence. Situated on the Silk Road, the city was an important commercial centre. The court at Nishapur attracted scholars from all over the Islamic world including the scientist al-Biruni (973–1050) and the mathematician and poet Omar Khayyam (1048–1131), famous for his collection of poems, the *Rubaiyat*.

During their rule, the Seljuqs completed many building projects, including *madrasas* (religious colleges), mosques, hospitals and caravanserais. Beautiful *muqarnas* or honeycomb vaulting was used to decorate many buildings across the empire.

The Seljuq sultans relied on the support of their viziers or advisors to govern. Many of these officials, such as Nizam al-Mulk (1018–92), were Persian. He famously worked for two sultans and wrote an important book, the *Siyasatnameh* ('Book of Government') on how to manage the empire, from employing mercenaries to collecting taxes, based on his own experiences.

Pottery bowl, painted with an enthroned Seljuq ruler and attendants. Kashan, Iran, 1187.

A few years after defeating the Byzantines at Manzikert in 1071, the Seljuqs also took control of Anatolia, with first Nicea (Iznik) and later Konya as their capital. Known as the 'Seljuqs of Rum', some rulers took their names from legendary Persian kings like Kai Khosrau, described in the popular epic poem the *Shahnameh* (the 'Book of Kings').

Silver *dirham* of the Seljuq sultan Kilij Arslan IV. Sivas, Turkey, 1248.

In 1243 the Mongols swept across Anatolia and captured Konya. The Seljuq rulers were forced to become their vassals. Within sixty years they had lost control of the region completely.

Brass ewer, Herat, Afghanistan, 1180–1200.

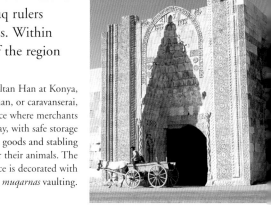

The Sultan Han at Konya, Turkey. A han, or caravanserai, was a place where merchants could stay, with safe storage for their goods and stabling for their animals. The entrance is decorated with *muqarnas* vaulting.

THE ZENGIDS AND AYYUBIDS

Portrait of Salah al-Din.

AD 1127 TO 1250 IN IRAQ AND SYRIA, SELJUQ princes had guardians called *atabegs* until they came of age. As the Seljuqs weakened, the *atabegs* grew in power and often claimed the regions they governed as their own. One such guardian, Zengi, was extremely ambitious. He seized Mosul in 1127, Aleppo in 1128 and Edessa in 1144, bringing them under his direct rule. His son, Nur al-Din, consolidated control of the region by adding Damascus in 1154.

Desperate to take over Egypt before the Crusaders, in 1169 Nur al-Din sent his commanders, including Salah al-Din ibn Ayyub (Saladin), a Sunni Kurd, to Egypt. In two years Salah al-Din had abolished the Fatimid Shia Caliphate. When Nur al-Din died, Salah al-Din became the first Ayyubid ruler of Egypt, Syria, Palestine, Yemen and parts of Iraq.

Detail of a woman with her servant, from a ewer made for the Zengid vizier of Mosul, Iraq in 1232.

Salah al-Din also created a unified, well-trained Muslim army that defeated the Crusaders at Hattin and retook Jerusalem in 1187. After a stalemate had been reached, he helped to bring the Third Crusade (1189–92) to an end by signing a truce with King Richard I of England.

Silver *dirham* of Salah al-Din, 1184–85, Aleppo, Syria

Painting of a battle beneath the walls of a town from Cairo, Egypt, *c.* 1200.

THE MAMLUKS

THE MAMLUKS, or slave-soldiers, overthrew their masters, the Ayyubids, in 1250 and took control of Egypt and Syria. Ten years later they became guardians of the holy cities of Mecca and Medina. From their capital Cairo and the cities of Damascus and Aleppo they developed a successful trading network.

Gold *dinar* of Sultan Baybars, Alexandria, Egypt, 1268. A prancing lion appears at the bottom of the coin representing his heraldic device.

Sultan Baybars (reigned 1260–77) was a gifted and able ruler. He defeated the Mongols in 1260 at Ayn Jalut (Goliath's Spring) in Palestine and so stopped them from advancing further west. He also campaigned against the Crusaders, and helped to destroy their remaining kingdoms, a task completed by Sultan al-Ashraf Khalili with the capture of Acre in 1291.

Mamluk is an Arabic word meaning 'slave'. Mamluks like Baybars were originally slaves from Central Asia and the Caucasus who served the Ayyubids. They became the first Middle Eastern dynasty to be based entirely on slave-soldiers. The sultans and officers had been bought and raised as slaves, and trained to be soldiers and administrators. This ensured that the men who served belonged to and were dedicated to the state.

The Mamluks took control of the trans-Saharan trade routes and acted as middlemen between South and Southeast Asia and Europe in the valuable spice trade and in the movement of other goods via Damascus and the Red Sea routes. The

A Mamluk servant. Detail from a 14th century ivory panel.

Spherical brass incense burner, Damascus, Syria, 1277–9. It was made for Amir Badr al-Din Baysari. It could be rolled across the floor between seated guests.

This mosque lamp made for Amir Sayf al-Din Shaykhu in the 14th century has the blazon or badge of a cup-bearer.

Venetians became the Mamluks' most important European trading partners. Textiles, spices, metals, pigments, glass, and paper all formed part of this rich trade.

The Mamluk dynasty had an important impact on art and architecture. With the trade-wealth of empire concentrated in their hands, Mamluk sultans and officers showed their rank and position in society by commissioning luxury objects. Consequently, woodwork, metalwork, ceramics, glass-making and the arts of the book flourished at this time.

Many objects made for Mamluk commanders are marked with a blazon. This 'badge' identified the service that a young Mamluk slave followed before he received his freedom. The cup of the cup-bearer, the pen-box of the secretary, the polo-stick of the master of polo are found on lamps, mirrors, bowls and many other fine objects.

Mamluk sultans are famous for the buildings they constructed in Cairo. Sultan Qaitbay (reigned 1468–96) was a particularly generous patron of religious architecture. His own mausoleum, which is now seen as a masterpiece, combines a *madrasa* (religious college), tomb and mosque. Banded and carved stonework decorate the walls, minaret and dome while gilding, black and white marble and stained glass bring colour to the interior.

From the mid-fourteenth century onwards, the Mamluk sultanate was in difficulties. Egypt and Syria suffered greatly from the plague epidemics of the 1340s and later. There were famines and raids by Crusaders, pirates and Arab nomads. Mamluk soldiers mutinied and in 1400 the Central Asian ruler Timur (Tamerlane) invaded Syria and sacked Damascus. When the Europeans opened up a quicker sea route to India via the southern coast of Africa in around 1500, the Mamluks lost their monopoly on trade with the East.

Ottoman expansion brought the dynasty to an end. After defeating the Mamluks near Aleppo in 1516, the Ottoman sultan Selim I occupied Syria and Palestine. The following year he invaded Egypt and defeated the Mamluks decisively.

A detail from a Catalan atlas showing Mansa Musa, Muslim ruler of Mali in West Africa. He travelled via Cairo while on the *Hajj* in 1324 and visited the Mamluk sultan at the time.

Mihrab and *minbar* in Sultan Hasan's mosque, Cairo. A *mihrab* or prayer-niche indicates the direction of Mecca. A *minbar* is a pulpit where an *imam* or prayer leader stands to give sermons.

Dome and minaret of Sultan Qaitbay's tomb.

THE ILKHANIDS

A painting of the siege of Khujand in Central Asia by the Mongols in 1220.

AD 1256 TO 1353 THE MONGOLS, a group of nomadic tribes from eastern Asia led by Chinghiz (Genghis) Khan, invaded Central Asia and northern Iran in 1219. They destroyed cities and massacred whole populations who would not surrender to them. When Chinghiz died in 1227, his lands were divided among his male relatives. In 1256 his grandson Hulegu Khan crossed Iran and went on to sack Baghdad in Iraq in 1258, killing the last Abbasid caliph, Mustasim. Hulegu then ruled Iran and Iraq with the title of Il-Khan.

The Ilkhanids, or Mongols of Iran and central Asia, ruled from Tabriz and later Maragha in Iran. From 1294 (when they converted to Islam) to 1335, the Ilkhanids maintained stability in the region.

A celestial globe. Possibly made in Maragha, Iran, around 1275–76.

This led to economic recovery and an artistic revival. Chinese scholars, administrators and craftworkers followed their rulers into Muslim lands. Close contact between China and the Ilkhanid world meant that Chinese goods were carried even further west and so were widely available in the Middle East. Chinese motifs such as the dragon, the phoenix and the lotus were copied on to local ceramics, especially tiles.

Manuscript painting showing Chinese sages bringing books on history to the Ilkhanid ruler Uljaytu.

THE OTTOMANS

THE OTTOMANS, named after Osman I (reigned 1299–1326) ruled the longest of the later Islamic dynasties. They were Turks in origin, who had established themselves in north-west Anatolia and raided Byzantine lands from around 1300. They first crossed into Europe in the mid-fourteenth century. In 1453 under Mehmed II 'the Conqueror' they captured Constantinople (Istanbul).

Bronze portrait medallion of Mehmed II by Gentile Bellini, 1480.

The Ottomans ruled through a strong centralized system of government in Istanbul, led by the sultan. From North Africa to Iraq, each part of the empire was ruled by a governor. Topkapi Palace in the capital was built as the centre of Ottoman government. Ottoman society was extremely ordered and an individual's profession and rank was indicated by their headgear and clothes.

Mehmed II and later sultans used slaves as servants of the state. Initially, prisoners of war fulfilled this role but in time the *devshirme,* or levy system, was set up. Under this, Christian areas of the Ottoman empire had to supply boys to help in the empire. Those boys thought suitable to be soldiers were trained for the famous janissary infantry regiments, while others were selected for the palace schools, and became officers and administrators.

Portrait of Suleyman 'the Magnificent' by Melchior Lorichs, 1559.

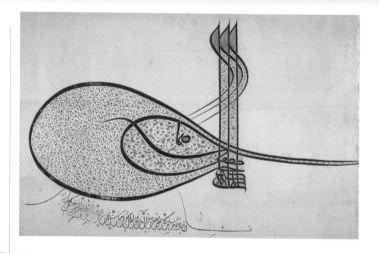

Tughra or monogram of Suleyman 'the Magnificent'. Ottoman Turkey, mid-16th century.

Mosque lamp made in Iznik, in Turkey, in 1549 for the Dome of the Rock in Jerusalem.

The Ottoman empire reached its height in the sixteenth century under Suleyman I 'the Magnificent' (reigned 1520–66). He was an extremely able administrator, improving the legal and tax systems, and keeping detailed records of all activities. However, it is for his military successes that he is often remembered. During his reign, the Hungarians were defeated at Mohács (1526), Tabriz in Iran was captured (1534–5) and his admiral, nicknamed 'Barbarossa', won a great naval victory at Preveza (1538).

Some of the most distinctive Islamic buildings date from Suleyman's reign. This 'Ottoman style' was developed by Sinan, his architect. Sinan (*c.* 1490–1588) was a janissary, probably from Greece, who had been conscripted through the levy on Christian villages. He started as a military engineer working on defence works, roads, and bridges before becoming chief court architect in 1538. Famous for the Suleymaniye mosque in Istanbul and Selimiye mosque in

Edirne, he designed hundreds of buildings across the Ottoman empire, working for three different sultans.

By the end of the sixteenth century, the Ottomans had created a huge empire including the Balkans in Europe, large parts of the Middle East, most of North Africa, and western Arabia. Although they had suffered a major naval defeat by the Holy League, an alliance of Christian European forces, at Lepanto in 1571, they were still probably the world's most powerful state at this time.

The Suleymaniye mosque, Istanbul, Turkey.

The decline began from about 1700. Territory was surrendered to Austria, parts of North Africa became virtually independent and trade was lost to the western Europeans. At the same time the Ottomans faced a new threat as the Russians built an empire. The challenge to Ottoman authority encouraged Greece and the Balkans to fight for and declare independence from the empire.

Amir Faisal (centre) at the Paris Peace Conference, Versailles, 1919. After World War I (1914–18), Faisal became king in Iraq, formerly part of the Ottoman empire.

The end of the dynasty came in the early twentieth century. After the German and Turkish defeat in World War I, the Ottoman empire was divided up by the victorious powers. The sultanate and the caliphate were abolished, and in 1923 the Republic of Turkey was born.

THE TIMURIDS

AD 1370 TO 1506

THE CENTRAL ASIAN ruler Timur (Tamerlane) took control of the region in 1370 and established his capital at Samarqand. He conquered Iran, Iraq, Armenia, Transoxania and northern India.

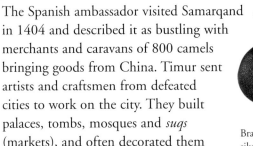

Brass jug with gold and silver inlay. Herat, Afghanistan, 1484–5.

The Spanish ambassador visited Samarqand in 1404 and described it as bustling with merchants and caravans of 800 camels bringing goods from China. Timur sent artists and craftsmen from defeated cities to work on the city. They built palaces, tombs, mosques and *suqs* (markets), and often decorated them with beautiful turquoise tiles.

Jade cup of Ulugh Beg, Central Asia, 1420–49. The Timurids controlled the main source of jade near Khotan in the Kunlun Mountains in Central Asia. Jade had been popular with Chinese rulers, and was believed to have protective and curative powers.

Like the Ilkhanids, the Timurids had a serious interest in astronomy. Ulugh Beg built an observatory at Samarqand in 1429. This observatory was a huge structure from which Ulugh Beg was able to study the sun, moon and planets and make extremely accurate measurements.

Timur's successors struggled to hold their western lands against Turkmen tribes and gradually the empire shrank. By 1470 the last Timurid ruled from Herat in Afghanistan.

The Gur-i Amir mausoleum in Samarqand, Uzbekistan, where Timur was buried.

THE SAFAVIDS

AD 1501 TO 1722

THE SAFAVID DYNASTY was founded in 1501 when Ismail I (reigned 1501–24), originally leader of the Safavi Sufi brotherhood in Ardabil, united Iran under his rule. The Safavids were Shia Muslims, and they made Shia Islam the state religion.

Safavid Iran's wealth depended on the export of silk. Shah Ismail I set up a number of workshops for dyers and weavers. Later, under Shah Abbas I, the production of textiles, including embroidered silks, brocades, satins and velvets, expanded greatly across the country. There were also royal carpet workshops in the major cities. Shah Abbas welcomed European and Indian merchants and ambassadors to Iran and so increased the silk trade from east to west.

Portrait of Shah Abbas I, painted by Bishn Das, Mughal India, *c.* 1618.

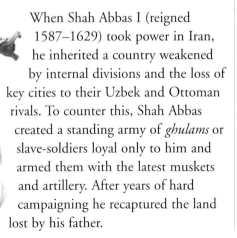

When Shah Abbas I (reigned 1587–1629) took power in Iran, he inherited a country weakened by internal divisions and the loss of key cities to their Uzbek and Ottoman rivals. To counter this, Shah Abbas created a standing army of *ghulams* or slave-soldiers loyal only to him and armed them with the latest muskets and artillery. After years of hard campaigning he recaptured the land lost by his father.

Safavid ewer with dragon-headed spout from Isfahan, Iran, 17th century. The design of this ewer was influenced by ceramics from India and China.

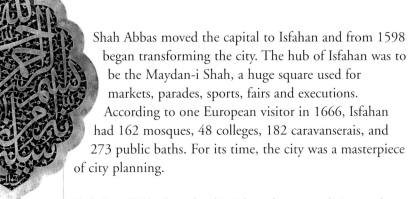

Shah Abbas moved the capital to Isfahan and from 1598 began transforming the city. The hub of Isfahan was to be the Maydan-i Shah, a huge square used for markets, parades, sports, fairs and executions. According to one European visitor in 1666, Isfahan had 162 mosques, 48 colleges, 182 caravanserais, and 273 public baths. For its time, the city was a masterpiece of city planning.

Steel door plaque, Iran, 1693–4. The inscription comes from the Quran and refers to the story of Suleyman (Solomon) and Bilqis (the Queen of Sheba).

Shah Ismail I had made Shia Islam the state religion and called himself the 'Shadow of God on Earth'. Because most of the population were Sunni Muslims, Ismail brought in scholars to spread Shia Islam. In his own show of faith, Shah Abbas I renovated the Shia shrines at Ardabil and Mashhad, and presented copies of the Quran and fine Chinese porcelain. Pilgrimage became very important and Shah Abbas travelled to Mashhad by walking over six hundred miles from Isfahan.

In 1722 Mir Mahmud, an Afghan tribal leader, captured Isfahan, resulting in upheaval in Iran for about eighty years.

The Mosque of the Shah, Isfahan, Iran, 1611–38.

THE MUGHALS

Painting of Akbar 'the Great' on horseback with a standard-bearer, India, *c.* 1585.

THE MUGHALS ruled over what is now Pakistan and large parts of India for over 300 years. Their empire was founded by Babur in 1526, when his forces invaded from Afghanistan and defeated the Sultan of Delhi at Panipat in India. Babur was followed by five other great Mughal emperors: Humayun, Akbar, Jahangir, Shah Jahan and Aurangzeb.

Babur (reigned 1526–1530) was known as 'the Tiger'. He came from Central Asia and was related to Timur and was also a descendant of the Mongol ruler Chinghiz Khan. Babur's descendants took the name 'Mughals' in memory of this.

Islam reached India in the early eighth century via Sind (modern Pakistan) but became established only in the eleventh century after the Ghaznavids from Afghanistan raided and then occupied the region. The growth of Islam in India followed, as many people chose to convert.

Gold *mohur* of Jahangir, with a portrait of his father Akbar, India, 1605.

This jade terrapin may have been an ornament for a garden pool in Allahabad, India, 1600–1605.

Portrait of Shah Jahan aged 36, holding a royal seal.

Gold pendant inlaid with jewels, Mughal dynasty, India, 17th century.

It was Akbar 'the Great' (reigned 1556–1605) who built the empire for which the Mughals became famous. Crowned at just fourteen, Akbar spent his reign reinforcing and extending his control through marriage, military conquest and careful diplomacy. By the time of his death, Mughal rule stretched over almost half of India.

In an empire where the majority of the population were not Muslim, Akbar realised he could only rule by co-operating with other faiths. In 1575 he declared the foundation of the *Dar al-Ibada* ('House of Worship'), in which Muslims, Christians, Jews, Zoroastrians and Hindus gathered together for religious discussions. In 1579 he also announced a universal faith, the *Din-i Ilahi* or 'Religion of God'. Although he was trying to bring together what he thought were the best aspects of these different faiths, some Muslims thought he was rejecting Islam.

Arts, crafts and architecture all flourished under the Mughals. The emperors particularly encouraged artists to paint, and their detailed work in miniature reveals the great wealth of the Mughal court. Rulers and courtiers wore clothes made from the finest cotton and silk, intricately embroidered and dyed with beautiful colours. Clothes were often embellished with exquisite jewellery. Fingers, heads, necks, wrists and ankles were adorned with diamonds, emeralds, rubies and pearls in gold settings. Imperial craftspeople worked hard to create these works of art in special workshops or *karkhanas*.